FIRST WEST YORKSHIRE BUSES

SCOTT POOLE

AMBERLEY

First published 2024

Amberley Publishing
The Hill, Stroud
Gloucestershire, GL5 4EP

www.amberley-books.com

ISBN 978 1 4456 9726 0 (print)
ISBN 978 1 4456 9727 7 (ebook)

British Library Cataloguing in Publication Data.
A catalogue record for this book is available from the British Library.

Orgination by Amberley Publishing.
Printed in the UK.

Contents

1

First Bus in West Yorkshire and York: A Brief History

First Bus was formed from a merger of two larger bus operations in June 1995, Grampian Regional Transport (GRT), based in Aberdeen, Scotland, and Bristol-based Badgerline. At the time they operated some 8,000 plus vehicles from Aberdeen to Cornwall. In 1997, the company became known as First Group and by 2001 simply as First. Perhaps in a radical shake up of the fleet, to ensure no fleet number duplication, the company introduced the five-digit 'Sema Voyager' numbers, in 2003. This system is still used today within the groups vehicles. During 1994–95, 926 new vehicles were ordered for the Badgerline group, which included seventy-eight Plaxton-bodied Dennis Lance saloons, with sixty-eight Dennis Dart midibuses. The first eighteen were bodied by Plaxton, the rest by Alexanders. Plus, ninety-eight Plaxton-bodied Mercedes-Benz minibuses. All for the West Yorkshire area, twenty-eight minibuses were later moved across to Manchester during 1997.

The Yorkshire Rider fleet was also being split into smaller operational subsidiaries, Bradford Traveller, Claderline, Leeds City Link, Kingfisher Huddersfield and Rider York. Each area would bring out a new livery, which was unveiled during the summer of 1995, with Bradford taking a two-tone blue livery, with around a dozen or so variations to the theme. Calderline opted for a pleasant white livery with blue and yellow relief colours; Leeds also ventured for a white base colour, but with red, orange and yellow relief colours. Huddersfield just used a variation of the current Badgerline Rider livery colours, as nearly seventy new buses were painted into these colours. York initially used a very pleasing cream and green relief livery, but then ventured for a drab green scheme.

By 1997, First had decided upon a new fresh corporate image with an off-white base colour with dark blue and magenta relief lines, along with a new interior décor, using a purple, magenta and grey colour scheme. Leeds had received a batch of new Volvo Olympians with Alexander Royale bodies, in the Leeds City Link livery, with the new interior design. 5606–21 were quickly repainted into the new corporate colours. By 1995/6 First were also looking into standardising the fleet image, as newer Scania and Volvo low-floor chassis have been placed on order with Wrightbus bodywork. These were mixed in with the large 926 vehicle order which was placed by Badgerline for 1995/6 delivery. Twenty-six Scania L113CRL chassis with Wrightbus bodies arrived in 1995/6 along with another six for delivery in 1997, for the recently awarded Park & Ride services within York.

First Bus still had over 200 plus former West Yorkshire PTE buses with Leyland Atlantean, Fleetline, Olympian and MCW Metrobus vehicles within the fleet. Plus, the remaining West Yorkshire Road car Leyland National and Olympians, most of which were working in York. However, by 1999, Bradford had withdrawn its remaining Atlanteans by the new year, along with the final PTE Olympians. This was because the Bowling Back Lane depot had managed to gain a five-year maintenance deal with Volvo, which saw B10BLE, B7BLA and B7TL chassis arriving into the fleet. The B7TL with Alexander ALX400 bodies were part of an order for 120 vehicles for Bradford, Leeds and York. Fifty-three Volvo B7L saloons arrived in York in 2000/1 along with forty-three Volvo B6BLEs shared between Halifax and York. The Volvo B10BLAs were based in Leeds, while the B7LAs were placed into service in Bradford.

As the new fleet standard vehicles with Wrightbus bodies with Scania and mainly Volvo chassis arrived, the final PTE chassis were withdrawn, with the Halifax Fleetlines going in 2001, after a farewell tour in the spring of 2001, the Olympians lasting until 2002. Bradford lost its Atlanteans in 1999/2000, while the Olympians were to last until around 2001. Huddersfield saw its Atlanteans withdrawn in early 2003, and the Olympians were also replaced around the same time. Leeds continued with Atlanteans until the final fourteen were withdrawn towards the end of 2003, although three continued until April 2004, with the last one bowing out in style on 22 May 2004. The MCW Metrobuses were all but gone by late 2003, with the final examples going in the spring of 2004, with PTE Olympians lasting until 2006.

The First group standard double decker from 2004 was announced as the Wright Gemini-bodied Volvo B7TL, with the later B9TL chassis, until 2016, with the arrival of the Mercedes-Benz-powered Streetdecks, these integral chassis with Wright Gemini3 bodywork. The standard buses were delivered new (Bradford and Leeds) or cascaded (Halifax, Huddersfield and York) from 2004. The standard First saloon is a mix of the Scania L113CRL chassis or the Volvo B6BLE and B10BLE, along with the B7 series chassis, all with Wrightbus bodies.

In November 2001, Leeds introduced the 'Overground' network of services, which were colour-coded and with a high frequency of ten minutes or less. Bradford, Huddersfield, Halifax, and York followed during 2002/3, again using front-line services for the new style of routes. Branding was key, as allocated buses were suitably adored, but some did stray from dedicated routes from time to time. Bradford did use a Sovereign standard on its major route the X6, which served Leeds, Bradford and Huddersfield. This standard was also placed onto other key routes in the city. The Flagship standard, which commenced in Halifax in 1993, later extending into the Huddersfield and York areas, offered the passenger standard of service with clean buses, friendly drivers and a much-improved frequency. The Gold and Sovereign styles were a continued improvement of the Flagship style.

Chairman Trevor Smallwood OBE and CEO Moir Lockhead OBE were both leading the group, with some passion and great ideas for the buses. In 2010 Tim O'Toole replaced Sir Moir Lockhead as the new CEO, while Martin Gibert became the chairman in 2010. He was in turn replaced by John McFarlane in 2015. Wolfhart Hauser was appointed chairman, as Mr McFarlane became the chairman of Barclays plc. Matthew Gregory was appointed as First Group Chief Executive after Tim O'Toole steps down from the position. During 2019 David Martin replaced Wolfhart Hauser as the group's chairman. Closer to home in Yorkshire, movement of fresh staff arrived in 2009 with the arrival of David Alexander, who moved from Transdev, who controlled the whole of the Yorkshire area. Meanwhile in February 2011, Giles Freanley, formerly a co-founder of Blazefield, became the MD for the whole of the First UK bus operation. Mr Freanley was succeeded by Janette Bell in October 2020, who was previously the CEO of P&O Ferries.

Giles Fearnley had the task of reshaping and branding the First image and improving the whole fleet, along with introducing a 'refreshed' group livery. The 2012 'Olympia' livery used pastral colours of the company, with lighter shades of magenta, purple and the main grey/white base livery. Around the same time a new blue and gold express livery was introduced. This particular scheme arrived in the West Yorkshire fleet from late 2016 on the X84, then the X6 and the X63. The Olympic year also saw an influx of ninety-eight new Volvo B9TLs, which were cascaded from the London 2012 Olympic special transport services.

Investment focused on both Leeds and Bradford as the years have shown, as both Halifax and Huddersfield fleets have had a small selection of new vehicles, as most were cascaded. However, in 2013 new Volvo B7RLEs were placed into service in both areas, along with a batch of Wrightbus integral Streetlites DF (Door Forward). The new integral Streetdeck debuted in 2016, Leeds being the major recipient of these vehicles, with Bradford gaining a batch for the

X6 service. By now the whole West Yorkshire fleet was being repainted into the 2012 'Olympia' refreshed livery. During 2014 a six-month trial of LT2, one of the eight prototype New Bus for London (NBfL) later known as the New Routemaster, had arrived in June. The trial was used to pitch against another green transport solution, the Trolleybus scheme, but ultimately both ideas failed, with planned investment for infrastructure, as the trolleybus had plenty of objections along the proposed route. The NBFWY was a bold idea, but it was quietly put to bed and no orders were placed for the new buses.

2016 saw the idea of the Bus 18 plan, where all operators in West Yorkshire would work together to improve the air quality, along with investment in new vehicles. This all came into reality during the early stages of 2018. When in Leeds the major players showcased their latest vehicles, with various in-service pledges and actions. This particular event saw the official introduction of the 'Leeds City' brand, as one of the Streetdecks was displayed in the new green livery. Towards the end of 2016, Huddersfield withdrew the last Volvo Olympians with Alexander Royale bodywork, as Alexander ALX400-bodied Volvo B7TLs were brought in to allow Huddersfield to become a low-floor fleet. Bradford also saw the same influx of low-floor vehicles, as the district looked to improve its fleet. Meanwhile across in York, the vehicles that arrived in 2008 were Volvo B7RLEs with Wright Eclipse bodywork. A batch of integral Mercedes-Benz Citaro articulated vehicles arrived in early spring 2009. Both batches were in a sliver livery. Cascaded Volvo B7TL/Wright Gemini double deckers arrived from Doncaster for the 66 University service, a contract awarded in 2016. In 2018 York City Council awarded First the contract for a five-year extension of the Park & Ride services. The two batches of Optare Versa-EV saloons arrived in 2014/15, which added to the issue of environmental credentials for the city. First York purchased a batch of twenty-one integral Optare Metrodecker-EVs, delivered in 2020/21. This new order saw the introduction of the dark blue and gold relief livery for the Park & Ride fleet. The Optare Versas and selected Mercedes-Benz vehicles also gained this new livery.

As the author of the book, I hope it brings many memories from employees of the company, enthusiasts, and the public. It has been another enjoyable venture through my personal archive of pictures. Take a pew, make a brew and sit back and sink into a nostalgic review of First West Yorkshire, including First York. All the photographs within this book were taken by the author.

The future and the past meet in Bradford on a special day during 7 November 2012, celebrating the last day of Leeds trams. Preserved Leeds City Atlantean PD R1/1 with Weymann bodywork, 331 was used for a day of photography in and around the city of Leeds. The tour commenced in Bradford, Hall Ings continuing forward to Leeds via Pudsey on the old 78 service. Pausing on the main A647 Leeds Road in Bradford, this was an opportunity to photograph 331 with one of the refurbished Hyperlink Volvo B7As with unique Wrightbus Streetcar bodywork. 19015 passes 331 during the morning run as it continues to Leeds Eastgate. However, since 2016 integral Wrightbus Streetdecks have been used on the main Bradford–Leeds 72 route. The current batch of Streetdecks arrived in late 2020 and were placed into service on the 72 during March 2022, with other routes also seeing the new buses.

2

Local Identity Liveries

Bradford Traveller brought a return to a traditional blue corporation livery for more modern Mercedes-Benz 709D with Plaxton Beaver bodywork, one of over ninety examples new in 1995/6. 2275 (N275 JUG) is seen in an area now known as Centenary Park, following pedestrianisation and building of restaurants and a feature fountain. 2275 was transferred to the Wyvern (Midland Red) operation in the year 2000 along with seven others from the Bradford allocation, 2264–70 and 2276.

5502 (B142 RWY) was one of six Roe-bodied Leyland Olympians which had to be completed by ECW in 1984. Leyland closed the Charles. H. Roe coachworks in Cross Gates, Leeds, during September of that year. The Olympian is parked up in Harrogate while waiting to return to Bradford working the former WYRCC 653 service.

During the summer of 1990, Yorkshire Rider took twenty-three dealer stock Leyland Olympians with Alexander R-Type bodywork for use in Bradford and Huddersfield. 5203 and 5207 were based in York for a short time before use in Bradford. Seen here in the old-style Knearsborough bus station is 5200 (G623 OWR) pausing for a short stay while working the 654 Sunday extension of the 653 service. By the middle of the 1990s the Huddersfield examples of the 52xx batch were moved across to Bradford.

This Northern Counties-bodied Volvo Olympian was one of ten to join Bradford in 1993, in two batches of five, 5401–5 and 5601–5. 5402 L402 PWR departs the Interchange Nelson Street exit for a little trip up to Clayton on the 637 service.

Bradford never really had a particularly standard livery, as buses would have variations to the theme. 5402 sports a simpler adapted scheme with an addition of a thin white band along the skirt and upswept at the rear.

Leyland Atlantean 6032 (GUG 539N) with Roe bodywork is seen paused on Centenary Way just opposite the Law Courts on a quiet summer's evening. The livery applied is similar to the style used for 5084, although 5084 had darker shades of blue.

This was the only original PTE Atlantean to gain this Bradford livery, as the other older vehicles would serve their final years in the Yorkshire Rider livery. 6032 was withdrawn in 1998 and scrapped in the same year at PVS in Barnsley.

5604 (L604 PWR), a Volvo Olympian with Northern Counties bodywork, is seen in the town of Otley working the 653 back towards Bradford. Sporting was to be one of the more bizarre versions of the Bradford livery – blue and cream with a couple of orange bands.

5204 also sported this particular version of the livery, which arrived during 1997, just before First decided on using a corporate fleet livery.

Hall Ings is the location for this shot of former WYPTE Roe-bodied Leyland Olympian 5111 (A111 KUM), pausing before heading off to Hirst Wood on the 640 service. By 2003 this Olympian became 30621 in the Sema Voyager fleet number series. The bus would also be painted into the non-low-floor faded magenta livery. However, by June 2006, the bus was withdrawn and scrapped in the Barnsley yards.

Former WYPTE Roe-bodied Atlantean 6352 (VWW 352X) was new in 1981 and lasted until early 2000, when withdrawn from service and sold to PVS for scrap. Here the bus is seen during November 1998, working the 618 service to Allerton, having just returned from the Holmewood estate. The bus sports the final version of the Bradford local livery, with additional white band. Initially based in the Kirklees district of the PTE, this bus was later transferred to Bradford after the first year of deregulation.

Another view of the unusual livery of blue, cream and orange applied to 5604. It is seen here of dealer stock Alexander-bodied Leyland Olympian 5204, working one of the B-series school contract services in central Bradford.

Experimental livery ideas were used on 1615, a Leyland Tiger coach, 5084, a Roe-bodied Olympian, and 5205, one of the Alexander-bodied Olympians. All three had three variations to the blue livery using a dark, light and a pale blue shade.

Keighley is the location for this shot of Volvo B10B with Alexander Strider bodywork, a style which was worked in conjunction with Yorkshire Rider. During 1993, thirty of this type of vehicle was shared between Halifax and Huddersfield. After a few years the batch was joined together in Halifax. 1005 (K105 HUM) travels down North Street in Keighley having about finished the very long Huddersfield via Halifax service. This bus became 60772 in the fleet-wide renumbering Sema Voyager series. However, the bus would be withdrawn during 2006, as First was looking to become a low-floor fleet.

During 1982/3 the WYPTE purchased twenty-two Duple Dominant-bodied Leyland Tiger bus chassis. 1662 (A662 KUM) was based in Huddersfield during her PTE days, but ended up in Halifax, as seen here with the bus working the 560 Commons service during 1997 without fleetname on the bus.

Late in the year 2000 the bus was withdrawn and sold to Sheffield-based Mainline, then moving to First Hampshire during 2001. By 2003 after passing between two dealers the bus was scrapped.

7254 (GNF 16V), a Northern Counties-bodied Leyland Fleetline which arrived into Yorkshire in 1997, was one of the final few remaining in the First Group fleet by 2001, in company with 7249 (BVR 71T), working to Shelf. 7254 is on the Illingworth route, while sporting the first version of the Calderline livery with upswept bands towards the rear, while 7249 is in the Yorkshire Rider livery with the Calderline fleetname. Halifax had a long association with Fleetline, from examples purchased in the 1960s to former GMPTE examples, fifty-three of which arrived in 1987.

This Northern Counties-bodied Leyland Fleetline, one of thirty-five such vehicles ordered by the PTE for delivery in 1979, 7073 (JNW 73V) was in fact the very last PTE Fleetline to be withdrawn, soon followed by the remaining former Manchester Fleetlines during 2001. 7073 was withdrawn in early July 2001. This bus is seen here working a special tour as part of locally based spring bus rally Heart of the Pennines. Fleetline 7140 (CWU 140T), a Roe-bodied Fleetline, is currently been restored within the Keighley Bus Museum.

3267 (M267 VWW) was one of fifty-eight Alexander dash-bodied Dennis Darts which arrived into the First Yorkshire fleet during 1995 in the new Rider Leeds livery. These were part of the large order for 925 buses purchased by the Badgerline company in 1994.

One of five transferred to Halifax during late 2001, with 3264–6 and 3268, it later gained the five-digit fleet number series. All the Darts would be painted into the simpler livery style adopted in the year 2000.

Fifteen Volvo Olympians with Northern Counties Palatine bodies had arrived just before the takeover announcement of Rider by Badgerline in early 1994. Seen at the entrance/exit to the newly built Halifax bus station, *c.* 1995, which won an award for design, is 5302 (L302 PWR). Twelve of the batch would leave Halifax bound for First Essex and the Eastern National fleet, as the batch became 4301–5,7–11, 14 and 15. Most were based at Colchester depot (4301–5 and 4307, 4309 and 4315) while 4308, 10, 11 and 4314 were based at Harwich. 5306 and 5312–13 remained in Halifax.

5120 (A120 KUM), a former WYPTE Roe-bodied Leyland Olympian, looks fresh from the paint shop as the bus pauses at the bus station exit, before heading off to the Mixenden on the 514 service. New in 1984, this Olympian remained in Halifax for all its operational life, bowing out in November 2007, with a one-way ticket to the Barnsley scrap yards. Many of the early batches of these Olympians were withdrawn by the PTE, most finding continued revenue-earning service in the UK, some going as far as Hong Kong!

New to Eastern National in 1980 as number 1927, this vehicle found its way up north during the 1990s, when it arrived into the Yorkshire Rider fleet. The bus spent some time with Quickstep Travel, as the firm was acquired by Rider Holdings during 1993. 1367 was later transferred across to Halifax during 1996 to become part of the new Calderline fleet. 1367 (MHJ 723V) is paused in Halifax before making the journey to Mixenden sometime during 1997. By the new year 2000, the National was withdrawn from service.

A small batch of Mercedes-Benz Vario 814Ds with Plaxton bodies arrived in early March 1998. They were intended for the Eastern National Group. All arrived in the yellow and green livery of Eastern National.

2401–4 were re-registered with West Yorkshire number plates before entering service. Here 2403 sports the Eastern National livery while working the 554 service. All the minibuses were very quickly painted into the Calderline livery within weeks of delivery.

1455 (G455 JYG) is one of ten Volvo B10Ms with Plaxton Derwent II bodies which arrived at service in 1990, five for Halifax and five for Huddersfield.

Huddersfield was home to 1450–5, which were regulars on the X37 express service to Halifax, with a twenty-two-minute journey time. Here the bus is seen working the 323 Meltham, in the Holme valley, in the 1994-inspired darker green Rider livery, with the 'R' seen clearly at the rear of the bus.

1995 saw major investment at Huddersfield in the form of sixty-six new vehicles: eighteen Plaxton Pointer-bodied Darts and forty-eight Plaxton Verde-bodied Dennis Lances. The new-look Yorkshire Rider dark green livery, along with Rider Huddersfield names, saw a selection of new buses displayed in the town centre. 3218 (M218 VWW) is the last of the Plaxton-bodied Darts, seen exiting the bus station bound for New Mill on the 316, a shorter working of the Parkhead service.

Holmfirth, *Last of the Summer Wine* country, sees one of the forty-eight new Plaxton Verde-bodied Dennis Lance saloons paused in the town's bus station. 4007 (M407 VWW) is in the new 1995 Rider Huddersfield livery with branding for one of the SwiftLink express services. One route went between Huddersfield and Halifax. The other would go to the latest shopping mall built outside of Leeds – the White Rose shopping centre. The 1995 deliveries remained in the Huddersfield fleet long enough to gain the faded magenta livery used for non-standard interior vehicles.

During 1994 six Alexander Dash-bodied Volvo B6Bs arrived at stock in Leeds. 3001–6 were soon transferred to Huddersfield and quickly repainted into the new livery. Here 3004 (L104 PWR) passes the bus station area heading through town on the 321 working the Bradley Circular service. Kingfisher was the new name for the Huddersfield operation when the Rider group was split into smaller units, although the new name did not stay for long. First after a year or so simply stuck with Huddersfield and everyone was happy.

Huddersfield had a very brief flirtation with a small batch of Wrightbus Access Ultralow-bodied Scania L113CRLs, 8432–37, which were transferred from York. They were initially used in the York livery but were soon repainted into the new dark green and cream livery.

Here 8433 (P433 YSH) pauses opposite the bus station working the 372 Almondbury service. These six Scania buses were used to promote the low-floor experience of the new fleet of these new buses.

The Leyland Atlantean AN68 with locally built Roe bodywork formed the main double decker for the Huddersfield fleet, with several PTE Olympians adding to the fleet. 6338 (VWW 338X) is paused at Holmfirth while working the 313, one of the Holme valley services, which is worked from Huddersfield to Parkhead, Holme, Meltham and surrounding villages. Huddersfield saw its final Atlanteans withdrawn during the early stages of 2003. 6294 has been preserved and is currently painted in the WYPTE livery.

York joined the Rider group in July 1990 along with Target Travel and Reynard Pullman. All three were combined to form York City Rider and later York. By 1997 the operation was named again as Rider York, as a new cream and green livery was introduced across the fleet. In a departure from Leyland products, York acquired eight DAF SB220LCs with Hungarian-built Ikarus Citibus bodywork, new in 1992. Here 1205 (J425 NCP) pauses on Rougier Street while on the Tang Hall service.

West Yorkshire Road Car took control of York City vehicles in 1934, working the service on behalf of the council, a situation which was to continue until 1986. By that time York was a separate unit from the main WYRCC fleet; AJS holdings renamed the fleet to York City & District, with a new blue and cream livery. Rider holdings acquired York in 1990, with a vast fleet of former WYRCC vehicles, as 5521 B523UWW illustrates, smartly repainted into the new York livery. The bus is about to depart the railway station stops working an evening service during the summer of 1997.

This Northern Counties Paladin-bodied Dennis Dart was new in 1995 to Greater Manchester, as 1107. The bus was part of a batch of seven buses for the network.

Seen here now as 3301 in the Yorkshire Rider Dart series of fleet numbers, on the main bus interchange area of Rougier Street in York, 3301 looks very smart in the new Rider York livery. It is working a local service 32 to Rawcliffe, which is near the Park & Ride site, one of seven sites offering free parking with cheap day-return fares into the heart of York City centre.

Rougier Street bus shelter sees the next York livery displayed by this former WYPTE Roe-bodied Leyland Olympian 5039 (CUB 39Y), seen here in 1998. By 2001 York would have its fleet painted in the new corporate willow leaf livery.

The service 30 would be put out to tender during 1999 and it was won by Stephenson's of Easingwold and remained with the company until early 2018, when the firm had withdrawn its services after some difficulties. The route is now operated by Reliance motor services.

In 1990, five Optare Delta-bodied DAF SB250LCs were purchased and used mainly on the 8 and 9 ring road services, deemed non-standard in Leeds. 1251–55 were moved across to York. 1252 (G252 JYG) is seen heading along Rougier Street, working the number 4 service and in the later two-tone green livery, similar to Leeds City Corporation colours. As for the number 4 service, it would see investment during 2006 as it became the FTR branded service with a purple livery and the batch of Volvo articulated vehicles.

The first of seven Plaxton-bodied Dennis Darts, acquired in April 2000 from York Pullman. The Easylink was a group of services operated by York Pullman, owned by Durham Travel services. The routes were school contracts and an open-top service. 3376 is seen parked near the Grand Hotel on Station Road in York, still in the York Pullman Easylink livery.

The Darts would be replaced by new Volvo B6BLEs during 2001–02, as Volvo would become the main chassis of choice for First Bus.

Leeds had a long-standing tradition with the Leyland Atlantean from 1965 until 1981, with a vast majority bodied locally by Charles. H. Roe of Cross Gates, Leeds. Here 6256 (PUA 256W) is paused on New York Street.

Leeds made a fresh approach to the new livery, with a white base colour, with red, orange and yellow, the finished livery looking smart on this Roe-bodied Atlantean. This bus became 30974 in the five-digit series. It was withdrawn in April 2004 and scrapped a month later.

West Yorkshire PTE took eighty integral MCW Metrobuses from 1980 until 1984, with a batch of ten vehicles bodied by Alexander, 7511–20. 7501–10 had the original MCW style of bodywork, while 7521–80 were the Mk II version. Here 7547 (A547 KUM) is seen during the summer of 1995 in Otley, working the 732 Leeds to Otley service, inherited from the sale of West Yorkshire RCC in 1990. 7547 was sold to Greater Manchester in 1996 (renumbered 5547). It returned to Leeds in December 1999, remaining with the fleet until withdrawal in March 2002, and then subsequently scrapped.

West Yorkshire PTE took to the new Leyland Olympian double-deck chassis with locally built Roe bodies from 1982 to 1984. An initial order for twenty buses for Bradford and Halifax was quickly followed with a repeat order for more, which went to Leeds. By 1985, the two PTE divisions had Olympians, 145 in total.

Here 5505, which was completed by ECW, when Leyland closed the Charles. H. Roe factory in late September 1984, is seen working the 15 service to Seacroft, a route that was later withdrawn. The Interchange was also redesigned during the late 1990s.

In 1990, Yorkshire Rider began to investigate seeing which vehicles would replace the time-expired buses. Two small batches of the new Scania N113 series double-deck chassis with Alexander and Northern Counties bodies arrived in 1990. Following a successful evaluation period, Rider decided to by another thirty-two Scania N113DRBs with Alexander R-type bodywork, which arrived in 1991 and continued into the new twenty-first century. Here 8032 (H632 VNW) is seen in the town of Ilkley working the 733, a former WYRCC service into Leeds during the summer of 1997.

As 1997 drew to a close, First had announced the details of the new corporate interior and livery designs, but an order for the Volvo Olympian with stylish Alexander Royale bodywork for Leeds saw numbers 5606–21 being delivered in the Leeds City Link livery. 5607 (R607 JUB) stands on New York Street next to the City Markets car park, a year or so before the redevelopment of the central bus station. 5607 had just entered service and is working the 15C to Seacroft. The bus looks impressive in the freshly applied Leeds livery. However, by the spring of 1998, the whole batch was repainted into the new First willow leaf livery.

A small batch of Plaxton-bodied Dennis Darts arrived in Leeds during 1997 painted in an overall red livery. Here 3314 (P827 YUM) is seen on Vicar Lane in the summer of 1997, just after the road became open to two-way traffic. The eight buses 3313–23 were soon transferred across to York to improve the Park & Ride services. 3314 left Yorkshire in 2001 and ended up working with the Avon area, while other batch members were sent into service at Glasgow.

During the year 2000, twelve Volvo Olympians with Alexander RL-type bodywork arrived from the Glasgow fleet. 5316–27 were based in Bramley when placed into traffic. Here 5318 (P194 TGD) is parked inside the old Skipton bus station during 2002 working the former 784 Leeds–Skipton service, which had become the X84 service. This batch of buses were transferred to Kirkstall depot, before being renumbered into the five-digit series as 30740–51. The influx of new Volvo/Wrightbus double deckers would see these buses replaced from 2004.

The Superbus guided busway was formally introduced during 1995, with thirty-five new Scania N113/Alexander Strider-bodied saloons, in the livery illustrated by 8635 (K1 YRL), seen here on Vicar Lane working the 71 service from Primley Park. The 45 to Shadwell and the 35 to Alwoodley all used the 500-metre track laid out on the outbound section of Scott Hall Road, from the Caribbean Cricket Club to the Potternewton Road roundabout. During the early stages of the new century two inbound tracks were laid from Wesley Drive to Potternewton Road. Unfortunately 8635 was badly damaged in a fire and the bus was withdrawn and scrapped.

Following the Huddersfield batch of Dennis Lances with the new Plaxton Verde bodywork would be a batch for Leeds, numbers 4049–78, all delivered in the Leeds City Link colours in 1996. Here 4054 pauses on New Briggate in Leeds working the north to south Leeds Roundhay/Middleton routes just outside of Lewis.

This area has now been changed into a cycle/pedestrian area with buses diverted to go up Vicar Lane and onto North Street. By the start of the twenty-first century, the Lances were replaced by Wright-bodied Scania and Volvo chassis.

3

The First Willow Leaf Livery

During 1998, Bradford had just completed a five-year deal with Volvo for maintenance of the fleet, which led to an influx of eighty-eight new buses from 1998. New buses were the Volvo B10BLE, B7LA and the B7TLs, removing the Atlanteans and leaving a mix of Leyland and Volvo Olympians, with a batch of Optare Solos. Here 1080 (W806 DWX) is one of the large influx of the Wright Renown-bodied Volvo B10BLEs, including the ten from Manchester exchanged for ten Volvo Olympian/Royales. 1080 also has the new style of line colour branding for key routes in the city, this the 620 Bierley service.

1048 (S667 RNA) was one of the ten Volvo B10BLEs swapped for ten Olympian/Royales in 1998 to help boost the Bradford fleet. Here 1048 is seen in Leeds working the 72 between the two cities, a route that can trace its origins back to the halcyon days of the tramcars. Fifteen more former Manchester Volvo B10BLEs arrived in 1999 and 2000.

First's long-lasting affair with articulated Volvos began in 1999, as Leeds had fifteen Volvo B10BLAs with Wright Fusion, with fifty-five seats inside these 18-metre vehicles. Here 1109 (T109 VWU) is seen in City Square working towards Cookridge on the 1C service. These vehicles were used exclusively on the Holt Park–Leeds–Beeston service, as the route had no really tight turns to contend with and there was no real alteration to street furniture. Although the number one would lose the Artics during 2010 in favour of conventional double deckers, some of the former Bradford Artics would work the route again in the new 2012 'Olympia' livery.

A year after the Leeds Articulated Volvos arrived, Bradford saw eleven Volvo B7LAs with Wright Eclipse Fusion bodywork arrive. These vehicles were used for the Pink Line services to Holmewood on the 618 route. 1124 (W124 DWX) is paused at the lights on Channing Way, ready to sweep into Nelson Street and park outside the Interchange and collect passengers for a run up to Holmewood. However, Bradford would lose its allocation of Artics, as they were transferred across to York to increase capacity on the improving Park & Ride services during 2004.

York also saw investment at the beginning of the twenty-first century with fifty-three Volvo B7Ls with Wright Eclipse bodywork. These were the only B7Ls for the Yorkshire fleet as the 2003 Volvo B7RLE would replace the B7L chassis. Here 1731 (YG02 DHN) is seen during a particularly dull and damp day in York, sporting the First willow leaf livery and new corporate interior colours and layout. The number 4 service would become part of the FTR Wright Street Car-bodied Volvo B7LA concept idea from 2006 until late 2012.

Since early 2023 the Otley services have been operated by ConneXions buses. Leeds and Bradford saw the Optare Solo arrive, six for Leeds which were worked by Kirkstall depot for Quickstep services, 2301–6, and Bradford had 2307–28 for use around the city. Here 2305 (S305 EWU) is paused at Otley working the W-series of routes, which served both Otley and Ilkley, until the return of WTPTA route numbers in the 900 series. The Solos were used on the extended 33 service to Otley via Yeadon, a change used from April 1990, after the sale of West Yorkshire Road Car. Most of the local services in Otley are now worked by Transdev as the Wharfedale Links initially using TransBus Darts. Then, following a rebrand in 2020, they used Optare Solos in a light green and cream livery.

Halifax gained twelve new Volvo B6BLEs with Wrights Crusader bodywork, numbers 3007–18. These were used on routes where larger buses would have difficulty with access. 3009 is seen on Orange Street working the 543 to Siddal service. The new 1998 willow leaf livery is shown well in this shot of the bus, without an advert to spoil the newly painted vehicle. York acquired numbers 3019–49 used on services around the York Network.

3359 (R722 HHK) is one of five Plaxton Pointer 2-bodied Dennis Darts new to First in Essex. These transferred to Huddersfield during 1999. Here the bus is seen near the bus station, working the 373 to Lindley, with route branding for the red line as well. Halifax also gained new Dennis Darts, five with Plaxton bodies, 3336–44, and eleven with Alexander ALX200 bodies, 3345–56, all arriving during 1998–99.

Bradford Interchange is the setting for this shot of Volvo Olympian with Alexander Royale bodywork 5628 (R176 HUG), part of a batch of eight vehicles delivered in the early stages of 1998. 5622–29 were used on the X6 and 72 services, with an occasional visit to Harrogate while working the 653 service. Bradford would gain another eight as numbers 5646–53 towards the end of 1998. Bradford had to wait for its next batch as ten Volvo B10BLEs were swapped for the next Olympians, as already mentioned in this book.

Leeds then gained another six Volvo Olympian/Royales as numbers 5630–35. These were arriving as the vehicles in the 5606–21 batch were being quickly repainted into the First willow leaf livery. 5632 is seen in winter sunshine as the bus makes a short peak time run on the 50A to Cross Gates, as the bus heads along St Peters Street. The West Yorkshire Playhouse new build forms the backdrop to this shot of the bus.

Halifax had two batches of the Volvo Olympian/Alexander Royales delivered during 1998/9 with numbers 5636–45 and the final batch of six, 5660–65. Leeds got five more with Alexander Belfast bodies on numbers 5654–59. Seen in full summer sun during 1999 is 5660, the first of the final batch of Royales, at Halifax bus station. It is working the very scenic 576 service to Bradford, which crosses the moors at Queensbury before dropping into Bradford.

New investment of the low-floor Volvo B7TL commenced in the year 2000, with 120 on order for delivery. Leeds had 5701–25 delivered first, as seen by 5716 (W716 CWR) working the 56 to Tinshill service. These new buses would be found on the 57 Barwick route and the 41 to Bramley depot services. 5716 is about to turn into Albion Street from the Headrow before heading north via Headingley towards Tinshill. Bradford had 5726–70 delivered, while Leeds then had 5771–5808, all delivered during the year 2000–01.

York gained, during 2001, Volvo B7TL/Alexander ALX400 numbers 5809–20, as part of the effort to improve the profile of the fleet, which at the time left Leyland Olympians from the old West Yorkshire RCC stock in the fleet. Here 5815 is paused at the railway station interchange stops while working the Acomb to Wigginton service 1, with full blue line branding.

First continued with both the Scania L94UB and N113 chassis all with Wrightbus bodies. Starting with 8101 through to 8143 and then from 8401–64. Most of the new Scanias were to replace the 8636–55 batch used on the guided busway with more modern vehicles, while others were used across Leeds. Some of the earlier 8400 batch were used in York on the Park & Ride services in the blue livery. Here 8457 (R457 JFS) passes through City Square bound for Primley Park, via the King Road Park & Ride site. Later in 2010 and 2011, these Scott Hall Road services would see demonstration and investment using the Hybrid Volvo B5LH double-deck chassis with Wrightbus bodywork.

4

The Faded Magenta Interlude

This livery application to an Olympian/Royale, this time in Bradford, as 30803 (R623 JUB) (5623) is collecting passengers while working the 637 Clayton service. The bus is in the faded magenta livery scheme and with full route branding for the 636/637 services into Clayton. Leeds also had some of its Royales painted into this livery. 5608, 12, 16–29, 39–40, 42 and 5646 were painted into the faded magenta livery during 2002/3. This means that 5608, 12, 16–21 would have had three paint schemes since late 1997. 5610 (R610 JUB) (30970) would be the only Royale to be painted into the 2012 'Olympia' livery.

New in 1996 to Capital Citybus, London, is this Northern Counties-bodied Dennis Arrow, which was designed from the Lance chassis. The Arrow was a gap between the Dominator and the successful low-floor Dennis Trident II chassis. Here 31902 (P402 PLE) (P902 HMH) is seen working the 97A service, returning to the bus station. Ten of these former Capital City bus Arrows arrived in Leeds during 2002, with 30579 (401), 30580–85(407–12) and 30586–8 (P413–15 MTW). Between 1996 and 2002 these vehicles were re-registered. 31902 later moved across to Manchester, along with the others in the same series.

Wetherby bus station was knocked down and rebuilt during the late 1990s, to make way for more housing and retail outlets, and behind the bus a restaurant is in the process of being built. 8012 (H612 VNW), one of thirty-two Scania buses delivered in 1991, pauses at the roadside stop before returning to Leeds, working the 98 service. Today this route has a mixture of hybrid and diesel buses working the services around Wetherby.

Bradford Interchange sees Volvo Olympian 5402 (L402 PWR), now 30755 with Northern Counties bodywork, making its way back to the depot on Bowling Back Lane. The faded magenta livery continued until around the early 2000s, as the fleet would become more low floor as newer Volvo and Scania vehicles arrived at service.

New in 1995 as part of the Badgerline order is this Alexander Dash-bodied Dennis Dart 3260 (M260 VWW), now 40629 in the Sema Voyager number series. The midibus has just been around the Morley area, as it returns travelling up Vicar Lane towards the terminus for the route. Opposite this Dart is one of the 1996-delivered Plaxton-bodied Lance 61012 (N474 JUG).

A unique vehicle which arrived in 1997 is 8656 (8995 WY) (M78WKX), a former Scania demonstrator vehicle. This Scania N113CRL has an East Lancashire European body, which was only used for a short time in the UK market. The bus arrived and was painted into the Superbus livery. By 2003 the bus was repainted into the faded magenta livery with its new fleet number 61134, as seen here on New York Street, working the 37 to Halton Moor service. 61134 was stationed at Cherry Row depot, the former BT area depot. It remained unique to the Leeds fleet.

The only former WYPTE Atlantean to gain the faded magenta-style livery was 6301 (30998), which for the entire summer of 2003 was out in service. In fact, fourteen Leeds-based PTE Atlanteans were used on many routes working from Bramley, Cherry Row and Kirkstall depots. Here 30998 is depicted on Park Row working to Fearnville on the 42 route during the last summer of operation. Most of the Atlanteans were withdrawn by March 2004, leaving 30990 (6310) to work on the last afternoon on the Pudsey 73 service, on 22 May 2004.

A special day was held in mid-November 2006, with the last remaining WYRCC ECW/Olympian in the York fleet. 30679 (3835) was used on a commemorative day around the City bus network. The West Yorkshire Information Service had hired the bus for the day and many haunts were visited by the vehicle. After the celebrations, 30679 was secured for preservation, and following a repaint into the NBC York livery, it was used again for another tour of York in 2007.

5

The Sema Voyager Series

The Sema Voyager fleet number series was brought into the First UK fleet to allow for easier fleet cascade of vehicles and one number per bus, which would reduce the need of duplicate numbers. Stagecoach also adopted the five-digit UK fleet-wide numbering system. First up in this particular chapter is the Leeds Articulated Volvo B10BLAs with Wright Fusion bodies, represented here by 10030 (V113 LVH), paused on the Infirmary Street stop for the number 1 service returning to Holt Park.

This was the first Volvo B7RLE with Wright Eclipse bodywork to enter into service in West Yorkshire. It arrived in August 2003. The vehicle became 66700 and is seen outside of the Queen's Hotel in City Square in Leeds. During 2012, 66700 moved to Manchester and then on to Chester, where the bus stayed, as Stagecoach Merseyside acquired the Chester operation. YJ53 HVC became 21255 in the Stagecoach series in 2013; however, due to fire damage the bus was withdrawn and scrapped in 2014.

61214 (YM52 UVK) is one of twenty new Scania L94UDs with Wright Eclipse Solar bodies from the batch 61214–33, all of which spent some time in Huddersfield during the initial stages of 2003. 61214 is seen departing the bus station working the 361 service. The whole batch was then sent across to Manchester to assist on Rail Replacement services for the West Coast Mainline group. After service with the group 61214 moved to Scotland as part of the Midland Blue Bird operation. Here the bus stayed until 2016, when it returned to Leeds, in the first willow leaf livery. By 2017 the bus was repainted into the 2012 'Olympia' livery. At the time of writing the bus is still working in Leeds.

Following on from the arrival of 66700 came the batch of fifteen (66701–15) Volvo B7RLEs with Wright Eclipse bodies, starting with 66701 (YK53 GXJ), seen at the Leeds City Rail station bus interchange, working the 5 to Old Farnley. 66701–9 arrived during December 2003, with 66710–5 arriving in April 2004. For West Yorkshire the B7RLE would become the standard single-deck chassis mixing with Scania L94 and L113 chassis, all with Wrightbus bodies, from 2002 onwards.

March 2004 saw the delivery of the initial First group standard double-decker bus, the Volvo B7TL with Wright Eclipse Gemini bodywork. 32431–73 arrived during 2004 until the B9TL chassis replaced the B7TL as the orders continued until 2016, with the introduction of the B5TL. Currently only the Hybrid B5LH is in the First West Yorkshire fleet. 32431 (YJ04 FYA) (K1 YRL) is seen brand new into service working the 16 Claret Line, the Pudsey–Seacroft service, looking very smart without adverts in Bramley Town end.

32469 (YJ04 FZU), a Volvo B7TL/Wright Eclipse Gemini, was one of the last to be delivered from the 2004 batch of these vehicles. The bus has just been placed into service as this midsummer 2004 shot shows, without advertisements. Here the bus is working to the Bramley bus garage. By this time the bus stop was placed opposite the bus depot, so the vehicles could turn around in the depot yard and return to service.

2004 saw continued deliveries of the now standard Volvo/Wright single-deck combination, as seen here with 66738 (YJ54 XVM) working in Halifax on 18 May 2010. Behind the bus is the stunning Halifax hilly enviros, as the town is set within a valley, allowing for some wonderful countryside vistas when travelling on rural services. Todmorden's Mill Wood depot was small in height. It saw in the later years the allocation of single-decker vehicles to the depot.

First continued with the low-floor single-deck orders as Huddersfield gained a batch of saloons from the 2004 order. Here Volvo/Wright 66747 (YJ54 XVY) is passing through Huddersfield town working towards Bradley on the 328 service. At the time Huddersfield still operated the sixty-six vehicles brought in by the Badgerline takeover, but in 2005 the town would also gain an influx of six-year-old Volvo Olympians with Alexander Royale bodies. These would prove useful on some of the adventurous hilly routes within the Huddersfield bus network.

On a wet 15 June 2012, Volvo B7RLE/Wright Eclipse 66763 (YJ05 VVE) is seen exiting the bus station in the town of Todmorden, just near the border with East Lancashire. The railway viaduct forms the background as 66763 turns out and heads towards Burnley, going through some very impressive countryside, before dropping into Burnley passing the Townley Park and Turf Moor, home of Burnley Football Club.

During 2008 York took delivery of a batch of Volvo B7RLEs with Wright Eclipse bodies, with the addition of roof advertisement panels, akin to the style applied to Belfast buses during the 1970s and 1980s. Here 69360 (YJ08 ZGN) shows off the new look in this elevated view of the bus proved by the historic Roman walls surrounding the city. The bus is seen on 30 July 2011 working the number 6 service to Clifton Moor, stopping at the Tesco supermarket, which is also handy for the Clifton Moor retail park.

During 2007 six Volvo Olympians with Alexander Belfast bodies were acquired by First for use in Leeds, as part of a new University service, 95 Unilink. The six buses, 31761–6, were painted in a blue livery with a dedicated branding style for the service, which ventured through Leeds and to the university. Here 31763 is seen on 21 April 2010, freshly repainted into the standard willow leaf livery, working the 33 to Horsforth, Fleece Hotel, the old terminus. These buses were also dual door. Having been moved from London, these were retained for the Unilink service.

First returned to the idea of operating articulated vehicles again in key areas of the UK fleet. Leeds, like Southampton, has a busy university hub, as has Sheffield. These areas all had the Unilink brand introduced during 2007, but Leeds and Southampton also saw the introduction of articulated vehicles in an orange and blue livery. Here former Bradford Artic 10040 (W128 DWX), a Volvo B7LA/Wright Eclipse Fusion, is seen entering the City Square loop while working the 95 service, which works to and from the Bodington Hall campus to the north of the city.

Ten Alexander Royale-bodied Volvo Olympians were transferred across to Manchester in 1998 in exchange for ten Volvo B10BLE saloons. 30244 returned to Yorkshire in 2009 after the bus had been repaired by East Lancashire following an accident. Here the bus pauses on East Gate bound for Seacroft during its stay in Leeds. By 2012 the bus was withdrawn from service and scrapped.

Having spent time working in the York Park & Ride services from 1996, the early Scania saloons were placed elsewhere within the West Yorkshire fleet. Here 8418 is paused on Boar Lane in Leeds while working the 35 to the leafy area of Alwoodley. The bus still has its guided bus way wheels attached. By 2011, following a trial period using a Volvo B5LH/Wrightbus Hybrid demonstrator, the Scott Hall Road routes would see changes during the next few years, as the 35, 45 and 71 became the 7 series.

Investment in the standard double decker for First during 2004 saw another batch arriving at the Yorkshire fleet. Here 32507 (YJ54 XTU) is seen exiting the redesigned Bradford Interchange on 29 April 2009, working the key route 363 between Bradford and Huddersfield with brown line branding. This route runs in conjunction with the X6, giving around a ten-minute frequency on both routes during the day.

Bradford and Leeds did see the vast majority of newer stock arriving into the First West Yorkshire fleet since the new standard Volvo/Wrightbus vehicle combination commenced deliveries. Here a typical First high-frequency front-line service sees 37057 (YJ06 XHM) paused on Hall Ings working the 645 to Greengates circular service.

The 72 Leeds to Bradford service via Stanningley Road has been part of the fabric of the transport scene since the tramways, even to the point of both Bradford and Leeds working through trams into each city. However, this was stopped as passengers change trams at Stanningley, but the motor bus saw through workings again, as both Bradford and Leeds corporations jointly operated the service. Bradford-based 37065 (YK57 EZU) approaches Hall Ings, arriving at Bradford centre working the 72 in the 2009 branding for the service, with the strapline 'Connecting the Cities'.

The X6 is a modern service which commenced just before the new deregulation era, using coach-seated former PTE Leyland Olympians in the Gold Rider livery. The route was operated by Bramley depot, then changed to Bradford, to allow for easier short service and emergency vehicle inserts across the route. Here Bradford-based 37083 is seen about to turn into the Interchange while working the X6 on 29 April 2009. The branding was the same style as the 72 service but with the strapline 'Connecting the Region'. The star in the destination screen indicates the service is a gold star service.

6

The Hybrid Interlude

From 6 July 2010 for around eight weeks or so a special demonstrator vehicle was used on the Scott Hall Road services, the 35 Alwoodley, 45 Shadwell and the 71 Primley Park routes. This Volvo B5LH Hybrid vehicle (BK10 MGV) used a small Volvo D5E engine coupled to a new Volvo gearbox, called I-SAM (Integrated Starter, Alternator and Motor) with a I-shift 12-speed transmission, linked to a parallel drive 70kw electric motor. It is seen posed at the Shadwell terminus of the 45 service, which works form the Infirmary Street stops, just off East Parade in Leeds. The bus would be given the fleet number 39200 on paper, and the vehicle was based at Bramley depot.

The first six Hybrid Volvo B5LH/Wright Gemini2 double deckers arrived in March 2011. By April the buses were placed into service in a new silver and magenta livery. Here 39203 (BJ60 BZC) is seen on the outbound section of guided busway on Scott Hall Road while working the 35 to Alwoodley on 9 April 2011.

Shadwell terminus is the location for the final member of the intital 39201–6 batch of Hybrid Volvo B5LHs, as 39206 (BJ60 BZF) pauses between duties on the 45. First was looking into integrating the three services into one whole series, which would allow better services for passengers along the routes. Fifteen more Hybrids would follow later in the summer of 2011, for the new 7-series and work on the X98 and 99 Wetherby services.

Although the 48 service ran to Wigton Moor, High Ash, shops during the day, night services were very few in 2011, so this was addressed by the extension of the 71 to serve the High Ash shops after the 48 service was stopped after 19.00 hours each day. 39205 is seen paused at the aforementioned stop at around 19.15, awaiting a return into Leeds. A few weeks after the new Hybrids had settled into service the next changes happened to the routes along the busway sections of Scott Hall Road. The 7-series was introduced to give a completely fresh look to the services and operate the Hybrids all along the three routes.

During the summer of 2011, another fifteen Hybrids arrived as 39221–35. These were quickly placed into service on the 7-series Alwoodley 7A, Primley Park 7 and Shadwell 7S services. Here 93224 (BP11 JWE) is seen approaching the King Lane Park & Ride site while working the limited stop peak time X7 express on 15 September 2011.

With twenty-one Hybrid vehicles now based in Leeds, the X98 and 99 Wetherby service saw some use by the Hybrids during 2011 and beyond. Here 39230 (BP11 JWJ) is seen in East Keswick, working its way back to Leeds, on 15 September 2011. The Hybrids continued working the 7-series and the Wetherby services across the years, but by 2016 the X98 and 99 service saw less of the Hybrids apart from an occasional trip out.

2012 brought in a new 'refreshed' First corporate livery, removing the willow leaf in favour of pastral colours and bands. The Hybrid livery took a few years to improve, but the livery arrived in the new colours as shown by 39233 (BP11 JWU). On 20 August 2015, the bus was caught working the 7-series service to Primley Park, wandering along Carr Manor Road, Leeds, sporting the new livery and local name for the bus operations around the UK.

During the spring of 2019, the first Hybrid was to receive the new Leeds City livery, without a corridor brand or front upper-deck flash of colour. Here 39204 (BJ60 BZD) works around the Alwoodley circuit, having just exited The Avenue onto Alwoodley Lane on 4 April 2019. This new livery returns the Leeds fleet to a two-tone green livery harking back to the Leeds Corporation colours used on the 'OMO' buses in the late 1960s to early 1970s.

During 2014 five original London HEV Hybrid vehicles were sent up to York to evaluate the type for the city services. 39001–5 were repainted into the new 'Olympia' livery and arrived in May, 39002–5 with 39001 arriving in October 2014. 39005 (LK58 ECZ) is seen working the 4 to Acomb as it approaches Clifford Street opposite the Clifford's Tower in York. This particular vehicle was used in a swap for a conventional standard First Bristol Volvo B7TL 37359 (WX57 HLZ), which arrived into York in March 2015, currently used for the 66 University service. Hybrids 39001–4 remain in York and continue to offer service in York, mainly on the number 1 Chapelfields , 4 Acomb, 5 Strensall and 6 Clifton Moor services.

7

The New Bus for West Yorkshire

June 2014 saw the arrival at Hunslet Park depot of a unique vehicle to the West Yorkshire area, LT2 (LT61 BHT, now LTZ1002), a New Routemaster. LT2 was one of the eight prototype vehicles delivered to Arriva London for trials on the 38 service Victoria to Clapham Common, via Hackney. LT2 will be forever recorded as the first of the New Bus for London (NBfL) to enter service on 27 February 2012, much to the amazement of the locals, as one bus attracted such local, national and international news. With service commencing, LT2 was soon off upon a world tour along with LT1 and 3, as production examples were placed into service on the 24 Hampstead Heath to Pimlico.

Upon arrival at Hunslet, LT2 was already painted green and with a couple of days being displayed to local MPs, staff and the dedicated drivers of the bus. Driver-type training began as plans for a huge consultation period were set, as LT2 was used to promote a new high-specification bus with triple-door boarding, new ticket ideas and other plans. LT2 is depicted in Huddersfield as the tour commenced.

September 2012 saw LT2 embark on a three-month tour of the key areas for where such a vehicle could be used to improve the passenger experience in West Yorkshire. Exhibited at the Eureka Halifax experience, LT2 was displayed along with senior Halifax staff to explain the new proposals to potential passengers. Leaflets were printed to encourage the public to offer their opinions on LT2 with an opportunity to deliver a new way of increasing passenger flow, with ticket options, and transform travel within West Yorkshire.

Early October 2012 and Brighouse and Hebden Bridge are the places to see this new bus. Brighouse was the morning stop and Hebden was the afternoon stop. The tour was attracting plenty of interest for the bus, as the public were able to sit, converse and ask questions about the proposal of the 'New Bus for West Yorkshire'. There was a general buzz around the vehicle, but with one major stumbling block: there were no plans to see the vehicle in service, which some of the public felt was a shame. That could have helped the proposal go futher, but Metro were concerned for the safety of passengers, as the triple-door concept was only just proving fine in London. Here LT2 is seen departing Hebden Bridge for a return home to Hunslet Park depot, via Halifax, the M62 and home.

Keighley and Dewsbury bus museums held open days in September and November respectively, with LT2 proving to be the main attraction at both. LT2 is seen arriving at the Riverside, home of the Keighley Bus Museum, for a day with the enthusiasts and a road run as part of that day's Regent bus celebrations. The bus was also used much to the appreciation of the gathered enthusiasts at Dewsbury's annual November open and running, with four return trips to Dewsbury and back.

Here LT2 is seen arriving at Woodhouse. With some careful manoeuvring, the bus was parked up and another day of discussions began. The Trolleybus scheme was also in the planning stages at this time, but was ultimately shelved because of funding and resistance issues. Despite great public interest and valuable comments and ideas placed on the leaflets, the idea, although solid enough, did not get the backing needed for funding and local council planning for bus stop investment. The whole project was concluded and LT2 was returned to London in early 2015. The bus was repainted and entered service working on the 38 route. First did work with Wrightbus, this time ordering the integral Streetdeck, with vehicles arriving in 2018.

8

The FTR Streetcar and Hyperlink

During 2005 Wrightbus designed and developed the impressive Streetcar, a tram-style articulated vehicle which could revolutionise public transport. The concept was based on the Volvo B7LA, 18.7 metres long and 3.7 metres high, and these buses looked fantastic with a tapered front end, giving that tram style to the bus. York was the first to gain these impressive vehicles for use on the University to Acomb number 4 service. 19010 (YK06 AUA) is seen on Station Road as the Grand Hotel forms an impressive backdrop.

York City Council worked together with First to improve the railway station interchange stops, with the removal of the taxi rank, which was in between the road and bus stops. Here 19006 (YK06 ATZ) pauses at the new stop during 11 May 2009, before heading towards the university campus. Despite the best efforts of both First and York Council, the FTR was withdrawn during 2012, with conventional double and single vehicles taking over the service.

Following the introduction to York, the FTR vehicles arrived in Leeds. Like York, the number 4 service was selected. The 4 service is a cross-city route serving Pudsey and Seacroft via the centre of Leeds, which saw the route change for the use of the Streetcars. Here 19023 (YJ07 LVR) exits the now former Leeds City rail station stops, into City Square, heading for Pudsey Waterloo, the terminus for the number 4 service at the time.

Whinmoor shops is the location for this shot of 19017 (YJ56 EAF) as the bus swings around the bus turning loop as it commences a journey to Pudsey Waterloo on 15 September 2011. These impressive vehicles were only six years old when it was decided that they were to be withdrawn, as the route these vehicles operated on was not really suitable unless major infrastructure design was to take place, thus improving the reliability of the service. However, such restructuring required investment, which at the time was not available. First withdrew the Leeds FTR fleet and then looked into a new way of using these expensive buses for a few more years.

Following the withdrawal of the FTR Volvo B7LA/Wrightbus Streetcars, most were chosen for an extensive internal refurbishment programme with an external repaint. A huge campaign began with bus stop posters and a special web page link to the new 'Hyperlink-72' service. 19028 (YJ07 LVW) was showcased on Briggate on Friday 26 October 2012 with its full 'Hyperlink' refurbishment and new interior design. On Sunday 28 October 2012, the day the clocks went back an hour, the new 'Hyperlink' service commenced, with 19015, 19009, 19028 and 19026 being the first vehicles out in service. Here 19004 (MH06 ZSW) (B7FTR) is seen working its way around Bramley town end roundabout heading towards Leeds on 14 June 2016.

Bradford Nelson Street on 21 November 2013 sees 19026 (YJ07 LVU) approaching the Interchange towards journey's end for the 72. The buses had to use the Nelson Street entrance and swing round to the stop within the Interchange, then exit via the Bridge Street entrance. In Leeds, these articulated Volvo/Streetcars had to venture round the Eastgate roundabout and stop outside the former Hogay's bar stop, where the layby was extended to accommodate these vehicles. However, by late 2016 the Streetcars' days were coming to an end as the new Wrightbus integral Streetdecks began to arrive.

9

The York Park & Ride Services

York City Council saw the potential of working with bus operators for a Park & Ride service within the city, thus reducing car usage. The first scheme commenced in 1990, from Tadcaster Road, now the Askham Bar service. Rider York, later First York, was successful in gaining the contract to operate the White line and Green line Park & Ride services from 1995. With this, new vehicles were purchased in the form of Scania L113s with Wrightbus Access Ultralow bodies – 8406–24 and 8425–31. 8408 (N408 ENW) is on Rougier Street in the two-tone blue Park & Ride livery.

During 1998, the McArthurGlen designer outlet shopping mall was opened giving shoppers even more out-of-the-city shopping, which was accessible by car from the A19 or via the 415 Arriva Selby–York service. During the year as the centre grew in popularity, both First and York City Council worked together to create the Red Line designer outlet Park & Ride. Here new Dennis Dart with Plaxton body 3343 (S343 EWU) is seen heading out to the centre during the summer of 1999.

First York, during 2003/4, decided to enhance the Park & Ride services by using more modern low-floor vehicles and giving the Park & Ride fleet a more improved profile. Here 60920 (1745) (YG02 DLU), a Volvo B7L with Wright Eclipse body, loads passengers for a return trip to the designer outlet on 28 August 2004. The bus also sports the improved First livery for Express and Park & Ride services, with the addition of more dark blue and route branding.

York also gained the batch of former Bradford articulated Volvo B7LA/Wright Eclipse Fusion 1116–26, as seen here with 10041 (1124) (W124 DWX). The new Park & Ride livery and brand was applied before the buses entered service, thus allowing a more modern and fresh approach to the Park & Ride service. At this stage Askham Bar, Clifton Moor (later Rwacliffe Bar), designer outlet and Grimston Bar were the current areas used for Park & Rides. By 2008 the network of routes would benefit from a complete influx of new Volvo and Mercedes-Benz vehicles, as these services continued to grow.

The Park & Ride contract was placed for renewal during early 2008; again First won the contract to provide the service. This time twenty-two new Volvo B7RLE/Wright Eclipse and fifteen Mercedes-Benz articulated Citaro 0350s were ordered. A new silver livery with large red city coat of arms was added to the visual branding. Here 69372 (YJ08 XYM) is paused on Rougier Street, taking passengers to the fifth site based near the Monks Cross shopping centre, which buses pass through.

The Volvo B7RLEs 69358–79 arrived between May and August 2008, while the fifteen Mercedes-Benz integral articulated Citaro 0350s 11101–15 arrived during January and February 2009. Here 11114 (BG58 OMK) is seen on 24 March 2009, freshly into service working the number 2 Rawcliffe Bar Park & Ride service. The bus is turning from Museum Street into St Leonard's Place as it returns to the former Clifton Moor named site. Both batches of vehicles also had new air-con systems, as seen by the roof pods on these new buses.

June 2014 saw the investment in six new electric vehicles for the Park & Ride services: the Optare Versa V1110-EV 49901–6. These buses entered service during the month of delivery, although they were supposed to be brought out earlier in 2014 – they had YD63xxx series registrations booked. Here 49901 is seen at Poppleton Bar, the newest of the Park & Ride sites, with six locations offering over 3,500 vehicle spaces. This batch retain the base silver livery, but with new branding showing their environmental credintials.

May 2015 brought in another six Optare Versa V1110-EVs into service: 49907–12. All were to have YJ14xxx plates, but these were surrendered for 15 plates. 49907 was used by parent company Ashok Leyland for a time. Upon return to the UK, the bus was reworked by Optare. 49907 returned to York, but was damaged by fire, repaired and returned to traffic in January 2016. 49912 (YJ15 AYO) is seen crossing from Pavement into Coppergate during 11 June 2015 working a short journey on the number 9 Park & Ride service to Rougier Street.

During 2016, York City Council placed the Park & Ride services up for tender. At the time certain criteria were not met. Upon this York City Council extended First York's current contract to early 2018. Bids were placed and the tender was subsequently awarded to First until 2025, who in turn promised new environmentally friendly vehicles. Here seen on Station Road is Optare Versa V1110-EV 49904 (YJ14 BHF) working the 59 Poppleton Bar service on 2 January 2020. The bus has received the new Park & Ride livery and branding.

Late July 2020, in the afternoon in the busy city of York, approaching Lendal Bridge is one of the six retained 2009-delivered Mercedes-Benz articulated Citaro 0350s. 11104 (BG58 OLV) was painted into the new livery at the beginning of 2020, without branding or the addition of the bronze finishing touches. The bus is seen working the 2A to Rawcliffe Bar during an afternoon run. York was about to have twenty-one new Optare Metrodecker-EVs delivered in the latter stages of 2019, thus giving the Park & Ride services a 90 per cent eco-friendly fleet. The Covid-19 pandemic caused the world to pause and also reflect upon those who had lost their lives to this worldwide virus. The loss of social contact for everyone would affect the population all around the globe.

After many months of waiting, the UK slowly had come to terms with Covid-19 and its effects upon society and daily life. The first of the much-anticipated Optare Metrodecker MD1110-EVs began an extensive period of daily driver training towards the end of July 2020. Here 39503 (YJ20 AXA) is paused on Station Road as the lights change to green, in the full new identity of the Park & Ride services, as this bus and 39504 are used on the day for driver familiarisation and training.

28 July 2020 saw only one of the recently delivered Optare Metrodecker MD1110-EVs working the Park & Ride services – 39502 (YJ69 CXC). This particular vehicle had arrived in February 2020 at York, and was used for some driver familiarisation until the UK entered lockdown on 23 March 2020. 39502 is seen turning from Micklegate into Skeldergate as the bus will then cross the River Ouse and turn into Tower Street. The remaining Metrodeckers were delivered during 2021 and are now fully in service across the city, some even working on stage carriage duties.

10

The Olympia Livery

2012 saw the introduction of the new 'refreshed' 'Olympia' livery, with a pastal colour pallet, using purple, magenta and the grey/white base colour. Giles Fearnley was MD of the First UK bus operations. In Leeds, Yorkshire, the first of the buses to be painted, 37103 (YN07 AYA), is seen on Roundhay Road, near Oakwood clock, working the 13 to Thorpe Lane in Middleton. The strapline 'WE believe in improving your BUSES' was spelling out the changes to come in the West Yorkshire and York operations.

Duncan Street in Leeds sees 37105 (YN07 AYC) turning from Low Briggate working the 3A to Gledhow, approaching Vicar Lane and the impressive Corn Exchange. This view of 37105 offers a look at the livery with a nearside and rear view. The initial 'Olympia' liveried buses had the strapline applied before the return of area names to the buses.

10 August 2012 sees a Bradford-based Volvo B7RLE with Wrightbus Eclipse bodywork, 69483 (YJ09 NYW), working the Pink Line route 617 to Allerton from Holmewood. The bus also had the route branding for this service, which are worked in conjunction with each other. The district name is just above the front door, with the stylised '*f*' next to it.

On 21 November 2015 37360 (YJ58 GNP) is going over the tops just outside of Queensbury, heading down to Halifax working the spectacular 576 service. It was a cold, bright and crisp day spent in Bradford as Transdev were launching their rebrand 'The Shuttle', and the recently repainted Volvo/Wrightbus into the former Bradford corporation livery was also out working the 576 on this particular day.

Bradford-based 60885 (1089) (W816 DWX), a Wright Renown-bodied Volvo B10BLE new in 2000, passes the Interchange while working the 620 to Bierley on a very sunny day on 9 April 2012, again with route branding and additional Metro sticker, informing passengers that all Metro tickets and passes can be used on this service.

Bradford-based 37068 (YN57 EZX), a Volvo B9TL with Wrightbus Eclipse Gemini body, heads down Sunbridge Road in Bradford. Working the cross-city service between Holmewood and Allerton, the bus has the new-style route branding with a larger front upper-deck window sticker. The bus has just been repainted and entered service without any additional advertisements, which gives the bus operator some additional funds.

A visit to Halifax on 30 January 2014 to see which vehicles had been repainted into the new livery and to catch other vehicles and operators. Here 37046 (YJ06 XLW) turns into Orange Street working a local service in the new 'Olympia' livery with side advert and district name applied.

A former Manchester Volvo B10BLE/Wrightbus saloon, new in 1998, was transferred to Bradford district in exchange for ten Volvo Olympian/Alexander Royale double deckers. 60820 (1053) (S677 SVU) was transferred over to Halifax during its life, as seen here with the bus working the 579 to Sowerby, a very pleasant area of the Halifax district. The side advertisement panel is occupied, hence why the district name is on the roof coving panel.

During the spring of 2013, Huddersfield and Bradford received and shared a batch of Volvo B7RLEs with new Wrightbus Eclipse 2 bodies. 69565 (BD13 NFO) is seen passing the railway station forecourt and bus stops as the bus heads for Bradley working the 328, with a cheery wave from the driver as the bus passes by. The livery is applied in a slightly different style on the front, but the district name is placed along the roof coving panel.

As Leeds gained ninety-eight former Olympic transport vehicles, older buses were quickly transferred across the other districts. Here Volvo B7TL/Alexander ALX400 30951 (5806) (YJ51 RRZ) is seen exiting Peel Street, working the 185 service to Marsden Hard End, just on the West Yorkshire Metro services border with services operated by Greater Manchester- and East Lancashire-based operators. More Volvo B7s were transferred across when Huddersfield started to withdraw the 1998 Volvo Olympians/Royales towards the end of 2014.

During the autumn of 2014, Huddersfield gained a batch of Wrightbus integral Streetlite DFs (Door Forward) for use in the area. Here 47499 (SN64 CHO) is seen working the 356 to Longwood as the bus departs the busy junction near the bus station.

Manchester, like Leeds, gained a large batch of the 2012 Olympic Transport fleet used by First across the highly uplifting London Olympics. Manchester saw the influx of integral ADL E40Ds into their network of services, which saw older buses being transferred to other areas. Here 37288 (MX07BSZ), a Volvo B9TL with Wrights Gemini bodywork, is seen exiting Peel Street working the 184 into Manchester, via Oldham. The bus is seen on 15 June 2012, just fresh from transfer from Manchester, with district name and the strapline still in place.

With the withdrawal of the final Alexander Royale-bodied Olympians, newer buses were selected to see a new branded image for the popular Holmfirth Connection routes. Here former Manchester 37298 (MX07 BUF), a Volvo B9TL/Wright Gemini double decker, is seen on 20 June working the 15.10 Peel Street departure to Parkhead on the 316 service. The bus has the new-style First route-branded vehicles, with painted line colour front end, white/grey middle and the 'Olympia' pastral purple colours at the rear.

A visit to York during August 2014 saw a selection of vehicles being repainted into the new 2012 'Olympia' livery. Here one of the seven late 2007-delivered Volvo B7RLE/Wrightbus bodies, 69276 (YJ57 YSM), is seen on Rougier Street working the 12 to Foxwood Lane. The bus must have just entered service as the district name is yet to be added. The bus has just been let out by the driver of 69374, one of the silver-liveried Park & Ride Volvos.

New to York as 5809 in 2000, then renumbered 30954, is YJ51 RDO, one of the 120 Volvo B7TLs with Alexander bodies. Here 30954 climbs up Station Road bound for Chapelfields service 1, outshopped in the new 'refreshed' livery with district name and side panel advert. By 2014 the remaining Alexander ALX400s would be withdrawn as newish former Doncaster-based double deckers were placed into traffic.

A batch of Volvo B6BLE/Wright Crusader bodies arrived in 2001/2, as 3019–49, these buses giving over twelve years of service. Here 40571 (3020) (YJ51 RKO) is seen exiting Rougier Street into Station Road working the 11 service to Bishopthorpe on 11 June 2015, a few short weeks before the type would be withdrawn, upon the arrival of the Streetlites.

Eleven former First South Yorkshire Volvo B9TL/Wright Eclipse Geminis arrived in 2012, again to try and withdraw older buses. Here 37248 (YN07 MKF) is seen working the Chapelfields service on 14 August 2013, passing through Station Road, with the minster in the background alongside the City Walls.

The service to the York University campus can be traced back to 2006, when a route commenced serving the major city centre transport hubs. K&J Logistics trading as York Pullman, a name long associated with Transport in York, used a traditional livery based around the former operator. However, by 2012, Pullman withdrew from the stage carriage services and these passed to Transdev. Transdev rebranded the Unibus service, retained the number and used more modern low-floor vehicles, but by 2014 the 44 service was up for tender and this was awarded to First York. Here 37068 (YN07 EZX), a former First South Yorkshire Volvo B9TL/Wrightbus decker, is seen turning into St Deny's Road from Walmgate.

During 2019, York gained a batch of former Greater Manchester Wrightbus integral Streetlites to replace the final Volvo B6BLEs within the fleet. Here 47476 (SN14 EAO) is seen on Station Road in a different version of the fleet livery, with the front end left without a colour. No doubt when the whole fleet has gained more of this new livery style the front end colours will appear.

Another batch of former Greater Manchester vehicles arrived during 2019 in the shape of the standard Volvo B79L with Wright Eclipse Gemini bodywork. Here 37445 (MX58 DZU) looks very smart in the newly repainted updated First livery, working the number 1 to Chapelfields service. York also has recently acquired a selection of former First Leeds Volvo B9TL deckers, with 37685 (YJ09 FVF) being painted into the above livery at the time of writing.

The White Rose shopping centre also has a reasonable bus station facility, so shoppers can arrive by bus, as seen here by 37105 (YK07 AYC), one of the first vehicles to gain the new 'Olympia' livery during 2011 into 2012.

First West Yorkshire continued operating the final remaining examples of the former Bradford district articulated buses. Here 10039 (W122 DWX), a Wrightbus Eclipse Fusion-bodied Volvo B7LA, is working the number 1 service back to Beeston. The bus is just in the process of exiting Holt Lane as it turns into Otley Road, before heading into Leeds, via Lawnswood and Headingley. 10039 looks brand new with the 'Olympia' livery and the fresh coat of paint applied. Since this picture was taken the articulated buses have been withdrawn and the new 2016 green-liveried integral Streetdecks arrived. Then during 2021/22 the junction seen here has been given traffic lights and new bus shelters on Otley Road.

After the successful London Olympics of 2012, Leeds received ninety-eight former Olympic transport vehicles for use across the network. These vehicles are the Volvo B9TL with stylish Wrightbus Eclipse Gemini 2 bodies. Here 36223 (BD12 SZZ) is seen working the 13 to Brackenwood on Middleton Park Road, an area where Aldi now have a supermarket. Behind the bus is the piece of land where the former Middleton Arms pub used to stand, which was once a terminus for the old PTE 20, 21 and 76 services.

September 2014 brought in a batch of smart ADL E40Ds for initial use on the 49 Seacroft to Bramley service. Here 33887 (SN14 TVV) is seen turning into Whitecote Hill from Leeds' Bradford Road, which was a major road through to Bradford before the A647 Stanningley bypass was built. This whole batch were based at Bramley until 2020, when some were transferred across to Halifax. These are used on the 508 Leeds to Halifax trunk route across the day.

2016 brought in several of the new Wrightbus integral Streetdeck double deckers into the fleet at Hunslet Park and Bramley bus depots. Seen here on 19 July 2016 is one of the Hunslet-based Streetdecks, 35203 (SL16 RGY), climbing the hill on Butterbowl Drive working the 42 to the terminus point. The Bramley-based Streetdecks were employed upon the 72 service, replacing the FTR/Hyperlink Volvo B7LA/Wrightbus Streetcar articulated vehicles.

An unusual working for the X84 on 9 June 2016 was this Streetdeck working the Otley to Leeds service. 35212 (SL16 RFX) is seen climbing the A660 Leeds Road, with the stunning backdrop of North Yorkshire behind the bus. The X84 was to gain some newer buses during November 2016, in the express blue and gold First livery.

The Leeds to Huddersfield X6 service commenced upon the advent of deregulation, using Gold Rider-liveried Olympians, then route-branded Volvo B7TLs. However, when the new express blue and gold Streetdecks arrived, the route was transferred to Bradford depot, then only to Leeds and Bradford, which made it easier for the whole route. 35229 (SK16 YOR) is seen exiting Vicar Lane while on a diverted route in Leeds working the X6 on 22 October 2019.

Following the splitting up of the X6 service between Bradford and Huddersfield, the team at the Old Fieldhouse depot brought in the express livery for a new service, the X63. The new service followed the former X6 express service from Bradford to Huddersfield via Brighouse. 32503–8 (YJ54 XTO,P,R,T,U & V), Volvo B7TL/Wrightbus, and 37083–37087 (YJ08 GVV, W, X, Y and Z), Volvo B9TL/Wrightbus, were all treated to the express livery and route branding for the X63. Here 32508 is seen heading towards Huddersfield in early March 2022, in full brand/livery for the X63.

November 2016 saw the introduction of a batch of ADL E40DMMCs branded for the X84 and painted into the smart-looking blue and gold express livery. The X84 is now part of the Hunslet Park depot, after the closure of Kirkstall Road, ending over 110 years of operation. Here 33481 (YX66 WKD) is seen at Draughton, a village just outside of Skipton, working the X84 hourly service to Skipton on 8 November 2016. At the time of writing this batch of buses was being transferred to First Wales.

Halifax still venture beyond their border in West Yorkshire into Greater Manchester and Burnley in East Lancashire. Litteborough, within the Greater Manchester area, is served by First, Transdev and Northern Rail, with good links to Manchester and other parts of the county. Here 69480 is seen working the 590 half-hourly extension through to Rochdale from Todmorden, as part of the Calder Connect brand. The 589 is the half-hourly extension to Burnley, using the same batch of branded vehicles, with green fronts and the roof cove branding.

11

City of Bradford

During the initial stages of 2022, a delivery of twenty-eight brand-new Wrightbus integral Streetdecks commenced for First West Yorkshire in Bradford. These new double deckers also arrived in a new tow-tone blue livery, not too dissimilar to the Bradford Traveller colours. 35644 (MD71 EOB) is seen on a wet 2 March 2022, having just entered service that week, working the 72 to Leeds. The new look to the Bradford fleet certainly catches the eye, as the bus is passing through Bramley Town End on the Bradford Line service.

Thornbury Roundabout has become a very busy multi-lane junction, with routes to Halifax, Bradford and Leeds passing through. Here 35639 is depicted working the 72 service towards Bradford on 7 March 2022, with a friendly wave from the driver.

Sunday 13 March sees 35660 departing the Eldwick terminus on the 615 to Bradford via Allerton, with a friendly wave from the driver. Two of the new buses were working the 615/616 Eldwick services during the day. Although the whole batch is supposed to be working the 72, X6 and X11 Bradford to Leeds services, a selection of these buses have also been seen working the 615, 622, 626, 640, 641 and 680 services, plus many other routes within Bradford.

During 2016, both Bradford and Leeds gained batches of the integral Wrightbus Streetdecks, with the latest bodywork by the Ballymena-based manufacturer. Here at the time of writing 35221 happens to be the only 16 plate Streetdeck in the new livery. The bus is seen arriving at Allerton terminus working the 617 service.

First West Yorkshire in Bradford has begun the repainting of the older fleet of buses, based at Bowling Back Lane depot, with Volvo B9TL/Wright Gemini double deckers. 37730 and 37071–5, at the time of writing, were in the new livery. Here 37071 is seen departing the Cottingley terminus to work the 680 service to Bingley, then returning to Cottingley before going into Bradford.

The Volvo B7RLE/Wright Eclipse saloon is, at the time of writing, one of two such vehicles painted into the single-deck version of the new City of Bradford livery. Here the bus is seen arriving at the Eldwick terminus, working the 619 service from Bradford. This area was once the preserve of the former West Yorkshire Road Car company, until joint working with Bradford Corporation up to Dick Hudson's pub, and later cut back to Eldwick.

Also on order for Bradford are ten integral Streetlite buses, which arrived during the hot summer of 2022. Here 63427 is seen at Tyersal having just commenced its return trip back into Bradford. This batch of Streetlites has more dark blue around the windscreen on the front end.

The former trolleybus turning circle at Thornton is the setting for this repainted integral Wrightbus Streetlite, a batch which was delivered to Bradford in 2015. Three of this batch so far have been painted into the new two-tone blue City of Bradford livery, introduced during March 2022. More of the Bradford fleet will gain the new Bradford livery during 2023, as repainting continues across the fleet.

12

Leeds City

20 February 2018 saw the showcase and introduction of the new livery and brand for Leeds, harking back to the days of Leeds City Transport with a two-tone green livery. Here 35266 (SL67 VMS) is seen turning into Westgate, Leeds, having been used on Victoria Gardens for a new multi-operator scheme and to showcase the latest in bus innovations. Leeds continues with the Wrightbus connection, but this time ordering over 200 plus integral Streetdecks.

On 21 February 2018, the red Headingley corridor routes were to see the first of the new Streetdecks arrive into service, with 35263 (SL67 VWO), 35268 (SL67 VWU) and 35280 (SL67 VXH) working the number 6 Leeds to Holt Park and 35273 (SL67 VXA) working the 28 Adel to Leeds Dock service. Here 35280 (SL67 VXH) is seen in the light of the setting sun working the 6 back into Leeds. It is turning out of Wood Hill Road into Tinshill Road, and looking very smart in the new brand and livery.

A tranquil location for this shot of 35275 (SL67 VXC), at the Adel terminus, which was once within the turning circle – recycling bins are in the old bus stop. Many years ago in the history of the Leeds bus services, the 28 was from Cross Green to Long Causeway, a road near the terminus, but the name changed to avoid some confusion. Today the route uses the same section between Leeds city and the terminus, but now serves the Leeds Dock area near the Royal Armories.

The Holt Park service can trace its origins to the creation of the Holt Park Village in the 1970s, a rapidly expanding housing project, which had a middle school, high school (Ralph Thorsby), Asda supermarket, sports and swimming pool, a sports hall and gym, and a shopping precinct and car park for the whole area to enjoy. The number 1 was originally the home for former Leeds City Transport Atlanteans, mixing later with PTE Atlanteans. Today, after many years with the Volvo B7 and B9s being used, the 2018 batch of Streetdecks were the new vehicles on the service. Here 35262 SL67VWN is seen turning into Holt Lane from Otley Road.

As the red Headingley corridor buses became the norm for the 1, 6, 28 and 97 services, the next buses were ordered for the blue corridor services, the Dewsbury Road routes 2, 2A, 3, 3A, 12, 13 and 13A. On 3 December 2018, one of the new buses, 35522 (SK68 TSZ), is seen travelling along Princes Avenue near Roundhay Park. Princes Avenue will be remembered by those who know of the Leeds Tramway, as this area had one of the reserved trackways up to the Roundhay terminus.

14 January 2019 was a very bright and crisp winter's day, which was particularly good for this shot of another Wrightbus integral Streetdeck, 35535 (SK68 TUP). Here the bus has just set off from Gledhow and is making its way back to Middleton, turning into Jackson Avenue, then onto Gledhow Lane and into Roundhay Road, near Oakwood clock. These buses, like the red corridor vehicles, have the USB power sockets, Wi-Fi, improved seating and audio-visual 'next stop' announcements. The screen in the upper-deck window is part of the Hanover display system with route details, passenger information and other helpful and useful traffic and travel news. Plus, a very cheerful wave from the driver, which finishes this shot nicely.

On 20 February 2019, it was an incredibly wet day, for the most part as this shot will show, at the Thorpe Lane, Middelton, terminus for the 2, 12, 13 and 13A. Here 35523 (SK68 TTE) is seen working the 13A to Gledhow, via Roundhay Road, in the opposite direction to the 3A. The Middelton services are interwork buses giving passengers choice and around a ten-minute headway before the next bus arrives at key points along the corridor.

The same day, 20 February 2019, sees a contrast in the weather with a brief spell of bright sunshine as the dark leaden sky behind forecasts more rain. Here 35550 (SK68 TTZ) is seen working the 2 service back to Roundhay turning into Acre Road. The bus will then travel along Bodmin Road, before joining Beeston Park Road and then onto the Ring Road and turning into Dewsbury Road at the Tommy Wass pub junction. The 13 and 13A will return to the Roundhay area via the Belle Ilse Road and on to the Hunslet shopping centre, while the 12 follows the same route as the 13 service.

June 2019 saw another batch of the Wrightbus Streetdecks arrive, this time with green fronts. The batch commenced revenue-earning service on the 49 Bramley to Monkswood Gate and the 50/50A Horsforth to Seacroft services. Here on 3 June 35569 (SK19 EZR) is seen turning out of Boggart Hill Drive into Kentmere Drive, heading towards the Seacroft bus station and retail area before making a return to Horsforth as a 50A.

Also seen on 3 June 2019 is 35582 (SK19 EZC), another integral Wrightbus Streetdeck, working the long service between Bramley bus station and Monkswood Gate. The buses used to service a stop opposite the Bramley depot, but a service revision saw the route curtailed to stop at the Bramley shopping centre stops instead. Here 35582 is completing the 49 as it has almost reached the Monkswood Gate terminus. From here the driver will switch off the bus, read his paper or catch up with social media, before setting off for the return trip back to Bramley.

On 17 July, more green front-liveried Streetdecks took to serving the Leeds city network, here seen taking a long turn out of Intake Lane on to Coal Hill Lane. Bus 35576 (SK19 EZJ) is working the long cross-city service 16 to Pudsey bus station from Seacroft, via the city centre and St James' Hospital. Intake Lane used to see the former 23 service terminate at a stop 35576 has passed. Where the houses are now situated there used to be open fields and the terminus for the former 610 Buttershaw service.

35573 (SK19 EZN) is also seen on 17 July 2019 working the evening shift on the 4 service between Seacroft and Pudsey, then extending to Highfield Green. Here the bus is seen turning off Waterloo Road and into Ingham's Avenue, before turning into Owlcotes Road and then to the terminus point.

After much uncertainty regarding the future of Wrightbus, which entered administration in 2019, the company was successfully acquired by Jo Bamford, who had a vested interest in the company via a hydrogen fuel cell vehicle project. In Leeds new bus 35603 (YE69 YFU) is seen turning out off Lea Farm Road into Hawksworth Crescent while working the 50 back to Seacroft on 4 December 2019.

The order for the thirty-five remaining buses was dispatched soon after the Wrightbus Ballymena factory reopened and outstanding orders were able to be processed and delivered. Here 35606 (YE69 YGO) is seen working the 49 back to Bramley bus station during the sunny afternoon of 4 December 2019. This batch of vehicles also have Yorkshire, Leeds, registration letters, as the original plates may not have been available for the batch.

The 14 service from Pudsey to Leeds goes via Armley and Bramley. Here bus 35613 (YE69 YGG) is seen turning from Armley Ridge Road into Raynville Road at around 15:35 on 4 December 2019, as the bus is heading for Pudsey. The sun sets with a slightly red sky and the moon rising from the pylon wires behind the bus.

The final two vehicles from the delivery, which was delayed by the administration period at Wrightbus, saw the vehicles arrive with yellow fronts. Here 35637 (YE69 YHA) is seen passing through on to Call Lane from Duncan Street and the Corn Exchange, working the 4 to Seacroft service. At the time both buses were placed into service without the Leeds City branding, when 35637 was seen on 3 January 2020. Little did anyone know what 2020 would bring and the huge changes within society thereafter, as the bus industry suffered along with the rest of the UK, Europe and the world's business, retail and leisure industries.

A selection of the 2016 integral Streetdecks are now being repainted into the new Leeds livery, some with green front ends. Others, like 35207 (SL16 RFF), are only getting the light green at the front with no colour. The bus slowly makes its way down Vicar Lane while working the 2 service to the White Rose centre. A selection of this batch have since moved to Southampton, but their stay will be short, as this operation is due to close in early 2023.

The final entry for the Leeds City chapter of this book is a Volvo B7RLE saloon with Wrightbus Eclipse bodywork. 69414 (YJ09 FXB) looks resplendent painted into the basic Leeds livery, without branding and side panel adverts. Here the bus is working the hourly service between Otley and Skipton, the 784, as at the time of writing the X84 goes on to Ilkley on the hourly departure. The 784 is the old West Yorkshire PTE system-wide number for the Skipton to Leeds service operated then by the West Yorkshire Road Car Company (WYRCC). The route was acquired by Yorkshire Rider in 1990, when the vehicles and services of the WYRCC were absorbed into Rider control. During the late 1990s it was decided to work the X84 as an express service from Leeds to Otley and then extend to Ilkley or Skipton.

13

Heritage, Demos, Trainers and...

During the latter stages of 2015, a single Bradford-based Volvo B7TL/Wright Gemini was selected to be painted into the 1946 Bradford Corporation blue and cream. Here 37732 (YJ09 OCD) is seen on a bright, crisp 21 November 2015, passing through Queensbury working the very pleasant 576 service to Halifax. Later this vehicle would be named Stanley King in honour and memory of the Bradfordian who knew plenty about the city's transport heritage.

Halifax depot teams also decided to dedicate vehicles in the colours of the former Halifax Corporation, such as with 37048 (YJ06 XLY). But with a little modern twist the Halifax colours are in fact the new First Olympia livery using the Corporation colours. The result is quite a smart-looking livery adaptation on a modern vehicle, which has been done very well. The bus is seen on Hall Ings in Bradford working the 576 service on 21 November 2015. 37048 has been named Geoffrey Hilditch in memory of the man who was the Corporation's final general manager, before the PTE took control.

During July and August 2015, another vehicle was chosen to gain a heritage livery, this time the former West Yorkshire Road Car Company. 37675 (1812) (YJ58 RTX), which was a regular on the X84 service, is seen in Horsforth working the 97 to Guiseley on 1 September 2015. This bus has since been moved across to Bramley depot. One hope is that this vehicle will be named in memory of the late Trevor M. Leach, for many enthusiasts a gentleman who knew his West Yorkshire RRC history.

During September 2018, there was much interest in York's James Street depot, which was organising quite an interesting repaint. A former Park & Ride Volvo B7RLE/Wrightbus Eclipse saloon was given a complete rub down, new panels and repainted into this Rider York livery. It was in this guise that 69374 (YJ08 XYO) was taken down to showbus alongside Hunslet Parks' (3)7674 (YJ58 RTV) in the Yorkshire Rider livery, dedicated to Brian Parkin. Here, a few days after its visit to Showbus, is 69374 working the Acomb 4 service on 2 October 2018, with the minster in the background – a classic York bus shot.

Bradford had a rather unusual demonstrator for a couple of months from June 2010: the Temsa Avenue, a lightweight integral vehicle for use of more rural services. Here as 63000 (YJ10 DFT), the bus is working the 607 service to Thornton as it arrives back towards the Bridge Street terminus. After its stay with First the bus moved to Centrebus and was later acquired by Arriva North East, who were the only operator to purchase the Temsa Avenue. The bus is still in active service with Arriva as their 4721.

During August 2013, York depot used this interesting ADL E350H demonstrator saloon, SN62DNJ, for a week on loan. The Hybrid E350H only sold in small numbers. If memory serves, First Essex purchased a batch of four in 2013. York used this hybrid across the main route network, as seen here with the bus turning into Coppergate working the 6 to Osbaldwick. The ADL E35H was discontinued in favour of the much-improved E20DMMC model and a potential new electric version of the E30D, which never caught on.

This vehicle is a former Volvo demonstrator on a B10BLE chassis with Northern Counties bodywork. It was with First in Hampshire and moved around some fleets before settling in York for a while. Here, across the River Ouse, is 66651 (K114 PRV) on a driver training course in York city centre.

Eastgate in Leeds is the location for this shot of 60877 (1702) (Y446 CUB), one of the fifty-three Volvo B7Ls with Wrightbus bodywork. First revised the training livery, using the main magenta and purple colours diagonally on the front and the current livery on the remainder of the bus, along with First standard driver training branding all around the vehicle.

Here V929 FMS departs Bradford Interchange, while on loan, working the main 72 Leeds/Bradford trunk service. This vehicle remained with Bradford until 21 August 2000. Bradford would receive the new low-floor Volvo B7TLs with the Alexander ALX400 bodywork, with numbers 5726–70 arriving during the summer of 2000, with new route branding and the colours for each high-frequency service.

During February 2017, this Yutong E12LF saloon was used for trials on First's Park & Ride areas against the current Optare Versa-EVs. The batteries are contained in the roof pod and in the engine compartment. With a 12-metre length and pleasant enough styling, this bus performed well during a visit. 62990 (YK66 CBC) is seen working on the popular number 7 designer outlet service, as it turns towards the railway station from Station Road.

Long before the Park & Ride tender was considered again for renewal, First saw an extension until 2018, which became the 2025 extension, when First retained the Park & Ride service. Speculation then began about which vehicles would be required for this new contract, with a few popular UK manufactures placed into the pot. Optare, who had built the Versa-EVs for the 2014/15 orders, dispatched a remodelled double decker to the city for an extensive trial period. 39500 (YJ17 FXX) was in fact new in 2014 and displayed down in London's Covent Garden, in blue. Here the bus is seen working the 9 Monks Cross service in the Heworth area, turning into Heworth Gardens from Malton Road on 14 August 2017.

June 2014 saw the PR1 service launched in Leeds, at Elland Road football ground, using three of the 2012 Volvo B9TLs covered in a green vinyl picture of grass. 36275–7 were chosen for the service until new buses arrived. They did arrive in 2018 in the shape of eight of the integral Wrightbus Streetdeck HEVs, as seen here with 35308 (SN18 XYE) turning into Vicar Lane working to Elland Road. The batch of buses are painted into the Leeds City livery but with the vinyls added on top. 35308 is seen on 19 August 2018.

Temple Green commenced during 2017, again using three buses from the initial batch of 2016 Streetdecks with correct branding vinyls. Just as the Elland Road route gained newer buses so did the Temple Green service. 35302 (SN18 XXY) is seen in the Leeds city livery, but with additional red vinyls for the PR2 route, as seen here as the bus turns into Mill Hill. 35801–4 were delivered in a red livery with white in between the upper saloon windows and lower saloon windows. 35805–8 were, as mentioned, in the full Leeds City livery, and all eight have settled into the Park & Ride services.

A third Park & Ride site was constructed at Stourton, an area outside of Leeds which was earmarked for use as a potential site for the proposed Supertram and Trolleybus schemes. As West Yorkshire enthusiasts will know, Leeds has regularly made bids for this form of transportation. During 2021 the Stourton site was complete and a new batch of integral ADL City-EVs were ordered and placed into service. Here 38403 exits Lower Briggate, turning into Boar Lane while working the service during 11 April 2022.

An unusual repaint at York was this former Leeds Volvo B7RLE/Wright Eclipse saloon, 69306 (YJ09 FWA), which was new in 2009. It was used to commence the X64 service in competition with the Yorkshire Coastliner Leeds to York section of their services. After the route was withdrawn 69306 was unbranded and then found its way to York, as seen here opposite the railway station. The bus was painted into the FTR purple livery, and it does look very smart as it heads for Acomb working the 4 service.

30790 was the last remaining Volvo Olympian/Alexander Royale in the Leeds fleet – well the only one to be given the new 'Olympia' livery. After developing a fault, the bus was placed into storage pending a repair and its future. At the time First were repainting the fleet into the 2012 pastral livery, and after the work was done on 30790, it was duly dispatched for a repaint. The results of the work are seen here on 16 June 2014, as the bus works the 50A to Seacroft. 30790 was the actual final Volvo/Royale in the First West Yorkshire fleet. It was withdrawn in September 2014 and acquired for preservation in November 2014 by the Keighley Bus Museum. 30790 was officially handed over in a specially commissioned photoshoot at Bramley bus depot during May 2015.

During early 2011, a brief visit was made by this Optare Tempo X1200 (YJ59 NNZ), which was used on the number 7 designer outlet Park & Ride service. Here the bus is seen approaching the railway interchange stops before returning to the designer outlet on 24 January 2011. The Tempo left York, as it was purchased by Norfolk Green of King's Lynn.

During the late August Bank Holiday weekend, York saw some new vehicles enter service, on a sleepy Sunday morning: 36501, 503, 505 and 502 worked the number 4 Acomb service. 36504, 36506-19 followed during the next month or so, with some single-deck Wrightbus/GBkites following in September with 63646 and 63653 working the 6 Clifton service. Here 36515 is seen working the number 1 Wigginton to Chapelfields service in early September 2023. This bus was also used by First South Yorkshire (Sheffield) in November 2023 as part of the electric bus trails in the city.

Acknowledgements

Again, I would like to thank Connor and Nikki, along with Phillip and all at Amberley Publishing, for their interest in allowing me to write four books about a subject known by plenty of fellow enthusiasts. The feedback on my previous books has been wonderful and encouraging. The information has been gathered by various means through personal notes, with key information from several issues of the *Metro Transport News*, *Leeds Transport Volume 5* and fleet books and fleet news from *Bus Handbook* and *Buses* magazine.

I would like to dedicate this book to all the drivers, fitters, engineers and back-room staff who have been kind to me across the years. Thank you for purchasing this book; I trust you will enjoy this little brief look at First West Yorkshire from 1995 until the present day. I have enjoyed sorting out photographs from my collection for inclusion in this volume. Just like the other books, grab a cuppa, biscuits, a comfy chair and look back at how First arrived and evolved.

During 2007 six Volvo Olympians with Alexander Belfast bodies were acquired by First for use in Leeds, as part of a new university service, 95 Unilink. The six buses, 31761–6, were painted in a blue livery with a dedicated branding style for the service, which ventured through Leeds and to the university. Seen here is 31761 (R922 WOE), paused on Park Row on 11 May 2009. On the front cover is Halifax 37047 (JY06 XLX), a Volvo B7TL/Wrightbus, working the 503 to Halifax, which later became known as the Zest brand for the route.